Sanjeev Kapoor

Recipes for Non-Stick Cookware

In association with Alyona Kapoor

Popular Prakashan
www.popularprakashan.com

Published by
POPULAR PRAKASHAN PVT. LTD.
301, Mahalaxmi Chambers
22, Bhulabhai Desai Road
Mumbai - 400026
for Khana Khazana Publications Pvt. Ltd.

First Published 2010
Second Reprint 2014

(4374)
ISBN: 978-81-7991-626-1

Design: Mahendra Ghanekar & Anjali Sawant
Photography: Alim Bolar, Bharat Bhirangi, Dilip Yande & Mangesh Parab

PRINTED IN INDIA
by Saurabh Printers Pvt. Ltd.
A-16, Sector 4, Noida

AUTHOR'S NOTE

Recipes for non-stick cookware are fast catching on in even the most traditional kitchens. Non-stick cookware has several benefits; the most obvious one being that food doesn't stick to the pan while cooking! But the most important one would be that non-stick cookware make it possible to cook food in very little oil or ghee, thereby cutting down on excess fat and calories. And let's not forget how easy they are to clean up!

Non-stick cookware come in myriad shapes and sizes, and have been customized for all types of cuisines. However, you can start with just the basics: a non-stick pan, a non-stick frying pan, a non stick *kadai*, and a non-stick *tawa*.

Here is my hand-picked collection of delicious recipes, which can be cooked up without any fuss, using non-stick cookware. Make delicious Malpua, or tempting Vazhakkai Chops. Try the Spicy Rajma Parantha, or Quick Stir-fried Noodles. Relish the Tandoori Subz Shaslik or tasty Sanjori.

And find out how you can marry tradition with convenience and good health!

Happy Cooking!

CONTENTS

NON-STICK PAN

NON-STICK FRYING PAN

NON-STICK TAWA

VEGETABLE VERMICELLI UPMA

INGREDIENTS

1½ cups vermicelli

1 medium potato, cut into ½-inch cubes

1 medium carrot, cut into ½-inch cubes

5-6 cauliflower florets

5-6 French beans, cut into ½-inch pieces

¼ cup shelled green peas

1 medium green capsicum, cut into ½-inch pieces

Salt to taste

2 tablespoons oil

½ teaspoon mustard seeds

6-8 curry leaves

2 teaspoons skinless split black gram

1 inch ginger, finely chopped

1 medium onion, finely chopped

2 green chillies, slit

¼ teaspoon turmeric powder

2 tablespoons lemon juice

METHOD

- Boil the potato, carrot and cauliflower in two cups of water in a deep non-stick pan, till almost tender. Add the French

beans and peas, and cook for another five minutes. Drain and cool.

- Bring five cups of water to a boil in another deep non-stick pan; add the vermicelli, salt and one tablespoon of oil.
- Cook for one minute or till the vermicelli is slightly undercooked. Drain, refresh in cold water and set aside.
- Heat the remaining oil in a non-stick pan and add the mustard seeds and curry leaves. When the mustards seeds begin to splutter, add the split black gram, ginger and onion. Sauté well till the onion turns light brown.
- Add the green chillies and stir. Add the cooked vegetables, capsicum and turmeric powder and sauté for four to five minutes.
- Add the cooked vermicelli and salt, and stir gently. Cook for five to six minutes.
- Remove from the heat. Mix in the lemon juice and serve hot.

CHEESY RICE-STUFFED PEPPERS

INGREDIENTS

1 cup grated processed cheese

¾ cup rice, soaked

1 large red capsicum, halved lengthways

1 large yellow capsicum, halved lengthways

1 large green capsicum, halved lengthways

2 tablespoons olive oil

Salt to taste

1 medium onion, chopped

2-3 garlic cloves, chopped

2-inch leek stalk, chopped

¼ cup tomato purée

½ teaspoon red chilli powder

½ cup American corn kernels

1 jalapeño chilli, chopped

METHOD

- Rub one tablespoon of oil and a little salt inside and outside the capsicum halves and set aside for about ten minutes.
- Heat the remaining oil in a non-stick pan; add the onion and sauté over medium heat for two minutes. Add the

garlic and leek, and continue to sauté for a minute.

- Add the tomato purée, chilli powder and salt, and cook over low heat for one minute.
- Add the rice and two and a quarter cups of water, and bring to a boil. Lower the heat, cover and cook till almost done.
- Stir in the corn kernels and jalapeño chilli, and cook for another three to four minutes, or till the water is absorbed. Add half a cup of the grated cheese and stir gently with a fork.
- Preheat an oven to 170°C/325°F/Gas Mark 3.
- Fill each capsicum half with the rice mixture and sprinkle a little of the remaining cheese over each capsicum.
- Place on a greased baking tray and bake for fifteen minutes or till the capsicums have softened slightly. Serve hot.

SHAAM SAVERA

INGREDIENTS

Kofte

500 grams spinach

2 green chillies, finely chopped

6-8 garlic cloves, finely chopped

3 tablespoons cornflour

Salt to taste

125 grams cottage cheese, grated

3 tablespoons oil

Tomato Gravy

2 cups tomato purée

1 inch ginger, chopped

5-6 garlic cloves, chopped

1½ tablespoons butter

6 cloves

4 green cardamoms

1 bay leaf

2 green chillies, chopped

1 tablespoon red chilli powder

½ teaspoon *garam masala* powder

Salt to taste

3 tablespoons sugar or honey

½ teaspoon dried fenugreek leaves, crushed

1 cup fresh cream

METHOD

- For the *kofte*, blanch the spinach in boiling hot water for two to three minutes and refresh in cold water.
- Squeeze out the water and chop finely. Mix together the spinach, green chillies, garlic, cornflour and salt to taste.
- Divide the mixture into twelve equal portions. Add salt to the cottage cheese and mash well. Shape into twelve equal balls.
- Flatten a portion of the spinach mixture on your palm and top with a cottage cheese ball.
- Bring the edges of the spinach together to form a ball (*kofta*).
- Heat the oil in a non-stick *kadai* and fry the *kofte*, six at a time, on medium heat for two to three minutes on each side. Drain and set aside.
- To make the tomato gravy, grind together the ginger and garlic to a smooth paste.
- Heat the butter in a non-stick pan; add the cloves, cardamoms and bay leaf. When they begin to splutter, add the ginger-garlic paste and green chillies;

cook for two minutes. Add the tomato purée, chilli powder, *garam masala* powder, salt and one cup of water.

- Bring to a boil, lower heat and simmer for ten minutes. Add the sugar or honey and the dried fenugreek leaves to the gravy. Stir in the fresh cream.
- To serve, cut the *kofte* in half and arrange in a pool of tomato gravy.

Chef's Tip: Before frying all the *kofte*, fry one to check if it holds its shape. If it breaks, add some more cornflour to the spinach mixture.

PYAAZ KI TARKARI

INGREDIENTS

8 large onions, sliced
2 tablespoons oil
1 teaspoon ginger paste
1 teaspoon garlic paste
Salt to taste
½ teaspoon turmeric powder
1 teaspoon red chilli powder
1 tablespoon Tamarind Pulp (page 95)

METHOD

- Heat the oil in a non-stick pan; add the onions and sauté till light golden brown. Add the ginger and garlic pastes and sauté till the raw flavour disappears.
- Add the salt, turmeric powder and chilli powder, and continue to sauté for two minutes. Sprinkle a little water and mix well.
- Lower the heat, cover and simmer for four or five minutes. Add the tamarind pulp and cook over medium heat for two or three minutes, or till the oil separates. Serve hot.

FETTUCCINE IN CREAMY PESTO SAUCE

INGREDIENTS

200 grams fettuccine (pasta ribbons)

1 teaspoon salt

1 tablespoon oil

Pesto Sauce

¾ cup (30-40) fresh basil leaves

3-4 garlic cloves

Salt to taste

3 tablespoons pine nuts

3 tablespoons olive oil

4-5 black peppercorns

¼ cup Parmesan cheese + for garnishing

To Serve

1 tablespoon olive oil

Salt to taste

5-6 black peppercorns, crushed

½ cup milk

Parmesan cheese, as required

3-4 fresh basil leaves, roughly torn

METHOD

- To make the pesto sauce, place the basil in a blender with the garlic and salt, and process for a few seconds.

- Add the pine nuts, olive oil, peppercorns and Parmesan cheese, one by one, processing after each addition, till all the ingredients are well mixed.
- Boil the fettuccini in plenty of salted water, in a deep non-stick pan. Add one tablespoon of oil and cook till *al dente* (cooked but firm to the bite). Drain, refresh in cold water and set aside.
- Heat the olive oil in a separate non-stick pan; add the pesto sauce and sauté for four or five minutes. Add the pasta and toss well so that the sauce coats the pasta.
- Stir in the salt and the crushed peppercorns. Add the milk and Parmesan cheese, and mix well. Add the torn basil and toss once again.
- Serve immediately.

Chef's Tip: If pine nuts are not available, use walnuts instead.

SPAGHETTI WITH MIXED VEGETABLES AND HERB SAUCE

INGREDIENTS

250 grams wholewheat spaghetti

1 medium carrot, cut into 1-inch round slices

1 small broccoli, separated into small florets

8-10 fresh button mushrooms, halved

1 medium green capsicum, cut into 1-inch pieces

½ teaspoon mixed herbs, roasted

3 tablespoons wholewheat flour

1½ cups milk

Salt to taste

¼ teaspoon white pepper powder

1 tablespoon parsley, chopped

METHOD

- Boil the spaghetti in five cups of water till *al dente* (cooked but firm to the bite). Drain, refresh in cold water and set aside.
- Blanch the carrot and broccoli separately, in one cup of boiling water

for two to three minutes. Drain and refresh in cold water.

- For the herb sauce, lightly roast the wholewheat flour in a non-stick pan. Add the milk and whisk rapidly so that no lumps form.
- Strain the sauce if required. Stir in the salt, white pepper powder and mixed herbs.
- In a non-stick pan, place the carrot, broccoli, mushrooms, capsicum and spaghetti, toss well and cook on medium heat for two minutes. Add the herb sauce and mix well. Adjust the seasoning.
- Serve, garnished with chopped parsley.

HARA MASALA PULAO

INGREDIENTS

1½ cups Basmati rice, soaked and drained
1½ tablespoons oil
1 inch cinnamon
4 cloves
3 green cardamoms
1 medium onion, thinly sliced
Salt to taste
3 cups Vegetable Stock (page 95)

Spice Paste

1½ cups chopped fresh coriander
8 garlic cloves, chopped
2 inches ginger, chopped
2 green chillies, chopped

METHOD

- Grind together all the ingredients of the spice paste and set aside.
- Heat the oil in a deep non-stick pan; add the cinnamon, cloves and cardamoms.
- When they begin to change colour, add the onion and sauté till light brown.
- Add the rice and continue to sauté for five minutes. Add the spice paste and salt, and stir-fry for three to four minutes.
- Add the vegetable stock and bring to a boil. Cook, covered, on low heat till the rice is completely cooked. Serve hot.

CHANAR PULAO

INGREDIENTS

400 grams cottage cheese, cut into 1-inch cubes

$1\frac{1}{2}$ cups Basmati rice

$1\frac{1}{2}$ tablespoons ghee

2 teaspoons sugar

1 large onion, finely sliced

1 bay leaf

1 inch cinnamon

2 cloves

2 green cardamoms

Salt to taste

METHOD

- Wash and drain the rice and spread out to dry. When completely dry, add half a tablespoon of ghee and the sugar and mix well.

- Heat half a tablespoon of ghee in a non-stick pan and sauté the cottage cheese cubes on medium heat. Drain and set aside.
- Add the remaining ghee to the same pan and sauté the onion on medium heat till crisp and brown. Drain and set aside.
- To the ghee remaining in the pan, add the bay leaf, cinnamon, cloves and cardamoms, and sauté till fragrant. Add the rice and salt, and sauté for two or three minutes.
- Add three cups of hot water and bring to a boil. Lower heat, cover and cook till the rice is tender and all the water has been absorbed.
- Add the cottage cheese cubes and stir lightly to mix. Sprinkle the fried onions and serve.

BESAN BURFI

INGREDIENTS

4 cups gram flour

2 cups powdered sugar

2 cups pure ghee + for greasing

½ teaspoon green cardamom powder

10-12 almonds, slivered

10-12 pistachios, slivered

METHOD

- Heat the ghee in a non-stick pan; add the gram flour and roast it on low heat, stirring continuously, for ten to fifteen minutes or till it starts changing colour and gives out a nice aroma.
- Add the cardamom powder, almonds and the pistachio slivers, and mix. Remove from the heat. Add the powdered sugar and mix well.
- Grease a tray with the ghee. Pour the gram flour mixture and spread it evenly on the tray to cool.
- Cut into square and diamond shaped pieces. Store in an airtight containcr.

NOTUN GURER PAYESH

INGREDIENTS

1 cup grated palm jaggery

3 litres milk

2 tablespoons Basmati rice, soaked and drained

1 bay leaf

5-6 green cardamoms

10 almonds, blanched and sliced

METHOD

- Boil the milk in a deep non-stick pan. Lower the heat and simmer till it thickens slightly.
- Add the drained rice and stir. Add the bay leaf and cardamoms, and continue to simmer on low heat till the rice is completely cooked.
- Remove the bay leaf. Add the jaggery and almonds, and simmer for five minutes more. Chill and serve.

GUR KA HALWA

INGREDIENTS

1½ cups grated jaggery

1 cup wholewheat flour

2 tablespoons pure ghee

½ teaspoon green cardamom powder

5-6 almonds, blanched and slivered

METHOD

- Soak the jaggery in one-and-a-half cups of water.
- Heat the ghee in a non-stick pan. Add the flour and roast on low heat till it turns reddish brown.
- Add the jaggery syrup and mix well. Cook, stirring continuously till the mixture begins to leave the sides of the pan. Stir in the cardamom powder.
- Serve hot, garnished with slivered almonds.

CORN PAN PIZZA

INGREDIENTS

4 four-inch wholewheat pizza bread

2 tablespoons olive oil

Tomato Sauce

2 medium tomatoes, puréed

4 tablespoons tomato ketchup

1 tablespoon olive oil

2 garlic cloves, chopped

1 small onion, chopped

Salt to taste

½ teaspoon sugar

6-8 black peppercorns, crushed

1 teaspoon oregano

Topping

1½ cups blanched American corn kernels

4-5 black peppercorns, crushed

2 cups grated mozzarella cheese

METHOD

- For the tomato sauce, heat the oil in a non-stick pan; add the garlic and sauté for half a minute. Add the onion and sauté till translucent.
- Stir in the tomato purée and cook till thick. Add the tomato ketchup and cook for another five to eight minutes.

- Add the salt, sugar, crushed peppercorns and oregano, and mix well. Set aside to cool.
- Heat half a tablespoon of olive oil in a non-stick frying pan and place a pizza bread on it.
- Spread a quarter of the tomato sauce evenly on the pizza. Scatter one-fourth of the corn over the sauce and sprinkle the crushed peppercorns.
- Top with one-fourth of the grated cheese. Cover the pan with a lid and cook on very low heat for ten minutes, or till the base has evenly browned and the cheese has melted.
- Cut into wedges and serve hot.

Chef's Tip: For younger children you can serve half a pizza per child or use baby pizza breads.

RÖSTI

INGREDIENTS

4 large potatoes, parboiled and grated

Salt to taste

1 tablespoon butter

1 small onion, finely chopped

METHOD

- Add salt to the grated potatoes. Mix gently without mashing completely.
- Melt the butter in a non-stick pan on medium heat and add the onion.
- Sauté for one minute and add the grated potatoes. Stir-fry till the moisture evaporates.
- Press the potato mixture down in the pan with a flat spoon or spatula.
- Cover and cook on medium heat for ten minutes till golden brown on one side.
- Turn carefully and cook the other side till golden brown. Serve hot.

VAZHAKKAI CHOPS

INGREDIENTS

4 (350 grams) unripe bananas

Salt to taste

½ teaspoon turmeric powder

20 curry leaves, chopped

1 teaspoon red chilli powder

1 teaspoon coriander powder

2 tablespoons rice flour

2 teaspoons Tamarind Pulp (page 95)

1 tablespoon oil + for shallow-frying

METHOD

- Peel and slice the bananas lengthways into three to four slices. Cut each slice in half if too long.
- Boil the banana slices in salted water to which the turmeric powder has been added, for five minutes. Drain and set aside to cool.
- Mix together the curry leaves, chilli powder, coriander powder, rice flour, tamarind pulp and one tablespoon of oil.
- Spread the paste evenly over the bananas slices. Set aside for fifteen minutes.

- Heat one tablespoon of oil in a non-stick frying pan and shallow-fry the banana slices, a few at a time, till crisp and golden on both sides.
- Add more oil, as necessary, to fry the remaining banana slices.
- Drain on absorbent paper.
- Serve hot.

Chef's Tip: Replace the bananas with sliced potatoes or yam.

DAHI KE KABAB

INGREDIENTS

250 grams drained (hung) yogurt

1½ tablespoons roasted Bengal gram, powdered

Salt to taste

2 teaspoons red chilli powder

1 teaspoon green cardamom powder

½ teaspoon cinnamon powder

½ teaspoon black pepper powder

4 tablespoons pure ghee

1 medium onion, thinly sliced

2-3 garlic cloves, ground

¼ teaspoon clove powder

METHOD

- Place the yogurt in a bowl. Add the roasted gram powder, salt, one teaspoon chilli powder, half a teaspoon cardamom powder, one-fourth teaspoon cinnamon powder and one-fourth teaspoon pepper powder and mix well.
- Divide into twenty equal portions. Moisten your hands and flatten each portion to give the kabab a smooth, even shape.
- Heat one teaspoon ghee in a non-stick frying pan and fry five kababs at a time till the undersides are a light golden brown. Flip the kababs over, drizzle one

teaspoon of ghee all around and fry till the other side is golden brown. Drain and set aside.

- Heat three teaspoons of ghee in the same frying pan and add the onion. Fry the onion till golden brown.
- Drain on absorbent paper and grind to a paste.
- Heat the remaining ghee in thc samc frying pan, add the garlic, remaining chilli powder, ground fried onions, clove powder, remaining cardamom powder, cinnamon powder, and pepper powder, salt, and sauté till the ghee separates.
- Add the kababs and gently mix into the *masala*. Serve immediately.

PANCAKE TRIANGLES

INGREDIENTS

⅓ cup refined flour

⅓ cup wholewheat flour

1 teaspoon baking powder

Salt to taste

1½ cups milk

4 teaspoons oil

Filling

1 teaspoon oil

2 spring onions, chopped

2 green capsicums, chopped

¾ cup sweetcorn kernels, cooked

Salt to taste

1 tablespoon tomato ketchup

METHOD

- For the pancakes, sift the flours with the baking powder and salt into a deep bowl.
- Add the milk and whisk well to prevent lumps from forming. Let the batter rest for ten minutes.
- For the filling, heat the oil in a non-stick pan. Add the spring onions and sauté for one minute.

- Add the capsicums, corn, salt, and sauté for one minute. Remove from heat and stir in the tomato ketchup. Set aside.
- For each pancake, heat one teaspoon of oil in a six-inch non-stick frying pan.
- Pour a ladleful of the batter and swirl the pan so that the batter spreads evenly around.
- Cook till the underside is lightly browned. Cook only on one side and remove.
- Place each pancake, with the cooked side down, on a flat surface and cut in half.
- Spoon a portion of the filling on one side of each half and fold over the other side to make a triangle. Press the edges down well.
- Serve immediately.

VEGETABLE SHAMMI KABABS

INGREDIENTS

200 grams yam, cut into 1-inch pieces

2 medium potatoes, cut into 1-inch pieces

1 large carrot, grated

10-12 French beans, finely chopped

¼ cup shelled green peas, coarsely ground

4 tablespoons split Bengal gram, soaked

1 teaspoon cumin seeds

1 inch ginger, finely chopped

2-3 green chillies, finely chopped

Salt to taste

2 tablespoons chopped fresh coriander

¼ teaspoon turmeric powder

½ teaspoon *garam masala* powder

½ teaspoon red chilli powder

5 teaspoons lemon juice

METHOD

- Drain the Bengal gram and transfer to a non-stick pan. Add the yam, potatoes and one and a half cups of water. Cover and cook till soft and completely dry.
- Heat a non-stick pan. Add the cumin seeds and roast lightly. Add the carrot,

French beans, green peas, ginger, green chillies and salt, and sauté on medium heat for two minutes. Transfer to a plate and set aside to cool.

- Grind the Bengal gram mixture along with the sautéed vegetables to make a smooth mixture.
- Add the chopped coriander, turmeric powder, *garam masala* powder, chilli powder, and lemon juice, and mix well. Adjust the seasoning.
- Divide the mixture into sixteen equal portions and shape into balls. Flatten lightly in the palm of your hand to form kababs. Refrigerate for an hour.
- Heat a non-stick frying pan and cook the kababs till golden brown on both sides.
- Serve hot with Coriander and Mint Chutney (page 95).

PAN-FRIED MUSHROOMS

INGREDIENTS

20-24 fresh button mushrooms, quartered

½ cup porcini mushrooms (optional)

½ cup oyster mushrooms (optional)

1 small red capsicum, cut into ½-inch pieces

1 small yellow capsicum, cut into ½-inch pieces

1 teaspoon olive oil

2 medium onions, cut into ½-inch cubes

3 garlic cloves, crushed

1 tablespoon soy sauce

1 tablespoon red chilli sauce

½ tablespoon vinegar

½ teaspoon dried thyme

Salt to taste

8-10 black peppercorns, crushed

7-8 fresh basil leaves, roughly torn

METHOD

- If using porcini and oyster mushrooms, soak them in lukewarm water for twenty minutes. Drain. Wash well and set aside.
- Heat the oil in a large non-stick frying pan. Add the onions and sauté over

medium heat till translucent. Add the garlic and stir-fry for a minute.

- Add the mushrooms, red and yellow capsicums, and sauté over high heat for three minutes.
- Add the soy sauce, chilli sauce and vinegar, and sauté for another two minutes. Add the thyme, salt and crushed peppercorns.
- Remove from the heat, stir in the basil and serve hot.

MALPUA

INGREDIENTS

1 litre milk

300 grams sugar

1 gram saffron threads

30 grams refined flour

½ cup ghee for frying

METHOD

- Cook the milk in a non-stick pan, stirring continuously, till it reduces to a consistency that coats the back of a spoon. Remove from the heat and set aside to cool.
- Reserve thirty grams of the sugar and make a syrup of one-string consistency with the rest of the sugar.
- Soak the saffron threads in a teaspoon of the hot milk and add it to the sugar syrup.
- Stir the flour and reserved sugar into the cooled thickened milk.
- Mix well and make a batter of pouring consistency, adding a little milk if required.
- Set aside for three hours. Heat the ghee in a non-stick frying pan.

- Pour a little batter into the hot ghee to form a pancake.
- Ladle the hot ghee over the pancake and turn it over. When both sides are cooked, drain and immerse in the saffron-flavoured sugar syrup.
- Serve warm.

ATHIRASAM

INGREDIENTS

¾ cup raw rice

½ cup rice flour

1 teaspoon green cardamom powder

¾ cup grated jaggery

4 tablespoons oil

METHOD

- Soak the rice in two cups of water for about two hours.
- Drain well and spread out on a piece of muslin in an airy place for twenty minutes.
- Grind the dried rice to a smooth powder. Add the rice flour and cardamom powder, mix and set aside.
- Boil the jaggery in half a cup of water till thick. Test the consistency of the syrup by dropping a few drops into a cup of cold water. It should be soft and sticky but should not dissolve in the water. Remove from the heat and set aside to cool.
- Pour the jaggery syrup, a little by little into the rice flour and knead into a soft, pliable dough.

- Divide the dough into twelve equal balls. Flatten each one into a thick round on a greased banana leaf.
- Heat one tablespoon of oil in a shallow non-stick frying pan and place six flattened discs in it.
- Fry till the underside is dark golden brown. Flip over the discs and drizzle one tablespoon of oil all around.
- Fry till both sides are dark golden brown and crisp. Drain on absorbent paper.
- Serve hot.

Chef's Tip: The size of *athirasam* can vary. Fry one disc first to test it. If it breaks while frying, add a little more rice flour and knead it into the dough. Prepare the dough a day earlier for a better flavour. If the dough is too stiff to shape, add a little milk and knead well.

BHAJNEE THALIPEETH

INGREDIENTS

3 cups *Bhajnee* Flour (see below)

1 medium onion, chopped

Salt to taste

½ teaspoon turmeric powder

9 teaspoons oil

METHOD

- Place the *bhajnee* flour in a bowl with the onion, salt, turmeric powder and one teaspoon of oil.
- Add the water, a little at a time, and make a soft dough.
- Divide the dough into eight equal portions. Flatten each portion into quarter-inch thick, four to five-inch rounds on a moistened banana leaf or thick polythene sheet. Make a hole in the centre of each *thalipeeth*.
- Heat a non-stick *tawa*, and spread half a teaspoon of oil over it. Transfer the *thalipeeth* carefully onto the *tawa*. Spoon half a teaspoon of oil around the sides and cook on low heat for one minute.
- Turn the *thalipeeth* and cook the other side for one minute, or till crisp and golden brown. Serve hot with a dollop of butter or yogurt.

Bhajnee Flour

1 cup wholewheat

1 cup rice

2 cups sorghum

2 cups millet

¾ cup black Bengal gram

¾ cup skinless split black gram

½ cup coriander seeds

Dry-roast each ingredient separately. Cool, mix and grind to a fine powder. *Bhajnee* flour can be stored for up to one month.

MYSORE MASALA DOSA

INGREDIENTS

3 cups *dosa* batter

1½ cups *Masala Aloo Bhaji* (*see below*)

2 medium onions, chopped

1 large green capsicum, chopped

2 large tomatoes, chopped

1 teaspoon red chilli powder

1½ teaspoons *chaat masala*

Oil for shallow-frying

4 teaspoons butter

Red Chutney

½ cup roasted split Bengal gram

7-8 garlic cloves

5-6 dried red chillies

1 tablespoon lemon juice

Salt to taste

½ teaspoon roasted cumin powder

METHOD

- Grind all the ingredients for the red chutney to a paste.

- Heat a non-stick *tawa*. Pour a small ladleful of the *dosa* batter onto the *tawa* and spread evenly with the back of the ladle to make a medium-sized *dosa*.
- Drizzle half a teaspoon of the oil around the *dosa* and cook over low heat for half a minute.
- For each *dosa*, spread a little red chutney all over the surface. Place some *masala aloo bhaji*, onions, capsicum and the tomatoes in the centre of the *dosa*.
- Sprinkle the chilli powder and the *chaat masala* and stir the potato mixture lightly.
- Add a teaspoon of the butter, stir and mash lightly with a potato masher, taking care not to damage the *dosa*. Spread the mixture all over the *dosa*.
- Continue to cook the *dosa* over low heat till the underside turns golden and crisp.
- Gently fold over one side and transfer the *dosa* to a serving plate. Cut into pieces and serve hot.

Masala Aloo Bhaji

4 medium potatoes, boiled and diced

1 tablespoons oil

½ teaspoon mustard seeds

2 teaspoons skinless split black gram

¼ teaspoon asafoetida

4 green chillies, chopped

10-12 curry leaves

2 medium onions, thinly sliced

1 inch ginger, grated

¼ teaspoon turmeric powder

1 tablespoon lemon juice

Salt to taste

- Heat the oil in a non-stick pan and add the mustard seeds.
- When they begin to splutter, add the split black gram, asafoetida, green chillies and curry leaves.
- Add the onions and fry till soft. Add the potatoes, ginger, turmeric powder, lemon juice and salt to taste.
- Toss well and remove from the heat.

TIKADIA

INGREDIENTS

1½ cups wholewheat flour

Salt to taste

4 tablespoons pure ghee + to serve

1 teaspoon roasted cumin seeds

½ teaspoon red chilli powder

1 medium onion, chopped

½ medium tomato, chopped

2 teaspoons chopped fresh coriander

METHOD

- In a large bowl, combine the flour, salt and two tablespoons of ghee. Add sufficient water and knead to make a soft dough. Divide the dough into four equal portions.
- In a bowl, combine the cumin seeds, chilli powder, onion, tomato and chopped coriander.
- Divide the mixture into four portions. Roll out each portion of dough into a thick three-inch disc and apply a little ghee on it.
- Place a portion of the onion-tomato mixture in the centre. Sprinkle a little salt.
- Gather the edges together and seal. Press and roll out into a thick *roti*.
- Heat a non-stick *tawa* and cook the *roti* on medium heat till golden brown on both sides.
- Serve hot, topped with a dollop of ghee.

MIXED-FLOUR ONION CHEELA

INGREDIENTS

2 cups rice flour

¼ cup wholewheat flour

2-3 spring onions, chopped

6-7 spring onion green stalks, chopped

¾ teaspoon ginger paste

2 green chillies, chopped

¾ teaspoon cumin seeds

Salt to taste

Oil for shallow-frying

METHOD

- Mix together the rice flour and flour in a bowl. Add enough water to make a smooth batter of pouring consistency.
- Leave to rest for half an hour. Add the spring onions, spring onion greens, ginger paste, green chillies, cumin seeds and salt to taste, and mix well.
- Heat a non-stick *tawa* and lightly grease it. When moderately hot, wipe it clean with a cloth. Pour one ladleful of batter onto the non-stick *tawa* and spread it with the back of the ladle as thinly as possible, into a round.
- Cook for a while and flip it over. Drizzle one teaspoon oil around and cook on both sides till golden brown. Serve hot with chutney or tomato ketchup.

TAWA PANEER CHAAT

INGREDIENTS

500 grams cottage cheese, cut into ½-inch pieces

Crisp puffed *puri* (as for *paani puri*)

1½ tablespoons oil

2 large onions, chopped

1 teaspoon ginger paste

1 teaspoon garlic paste

3-4 green chillies, seeded and chopped

¾ cup tomato purée

3-4 tablespoons *pav bhaji masala*

Salt to taste

½ tablespoon *chaat masala*

2-3 tablespoons chopped fresh coriander

METHOD

- Heat the oil on a non-stick *tawa*; add the onions and sauté till brown. Add the ginger and garlic pastes, and continue to sauté for a few minutes.
- Add a little water and continue to sauté for one minute. Add the green chillies and sauté for another minute.
- Add the tomato purée, *pav bhaji masala*, salt and the *chaat masala*, and continue to cook over a low heat till the oil separates from the *masala*.
- Add the cubed cottage cheese and half the chopped coriander, and stir gently to mix. Check the seasoning and cook over a low heat for two minutes.
- Make small holes in each *puri* and stuff with the cottage cheese mixture.
- Serve, garnished with the remaining chopped coriander.

HARIYALI TIKKI WITH CHOLE

INGREDIENTS

Tikki

500 grams spinach, blanched and chopped
4 medium potatoes, boiled and mashed
½ teaspoon red chilli powder
½ teaspoon roasted cumin powder
2 tablespoons cornflour
Salt to taste
4 teaspoons oil

Chole

1 cup chickpeas, soaked
1 large onion, chopped
3-4 green chillies
1 tablespoon coriander powder
1 teaspoon red chilli powder
½ teaspoon turmeric powder
1 teaspoon *garam masala* powder
1 tablespoon oil
1 medium tomato, chopped
Salt to taste

To Serve

1 medium onion, chopped
1 medium tomato, chopped
1 tablespoon chopped fresh coriander

METHOD

- For the *tikki*, mix together the spinach, potatoes, chilli powder, cumin powder, cornflour and salt. Divide into eight portions and shape into round *tikki*.
- Heat one teaspoon of oil in a non-stick *tawa* on medium heat and place four *tikki* in it. Fry till the undersides turn golden brown.
- Flip over, drizzle one teaspoon of oil all around and fry till both sides are evenly browned. Drain on absorbent paper.

- For the *chole*, boil or pressure-cook the chickpeas in sufficient water till tender. Drain and reserve the liquid.
- Grind together the onion, green chillies, coriander powder, chilli powder, turmeric powder and *garam masala* powder.
- Heat the oil in a non-stick *kadai* on medium heat. Add the ground paste and sauté for five to eight minutes or till well browned.
- Add the tomato and salt, stir well and cook till the oil separates. Add the chickpeas and cook for about five minutes. Add one cup of the reserved liquid in which the chickpeas were cooked.
- Stir well, and boil for two minutes. Remove from the heat.
- To serve, arrange the *tikki* on a plate. Top with the *chole*, sprinkle the onion, tomato and the chopped coriander.
- Serve hot.

CHEESY SPINACH QUESADILLAS

INGREDIENTS

1/4 cup grated processed cheese

700 grams spinach, blanched and chopped

1 1/2 cups wholewheat flour

Salt to taste

2 tablespoons + 5 teaspoons oil

2 garlic cloves, chopped

2 green chillies, finely chopped

1/2 teaspoon *garam masala* powder

METHOD

- Mix the flour with the salt and two tablespoons of oil. Add sufficient water and knead to make a soft dough.
- Divide into four portions and roll out each portion into a thin *chapati*. Heat a non-stick *tawa*, roast each *chapati* lightly and set aside.
- For the filling, heat one teaspoon of oil in a non-stick pan. Add the garlic and sauté for a minute. Add the spinach, green chillies, salt and *garam masala* powder, and mix well.
- Heat each *chapati* on a non-stick *tawa*. Spread half the spinach mixture over it and top with half the cheese. Place another *chapati* on top.
- Drizzle one teaspoon oil all around and cook for a few minutes. Flip over and drizzle one teaspoon oil all around again.
- Cook till both sides are evenly golden brown and crisp.
- Cut into wedges and serve hot.

TANDOORI SUBZ SHASLIK

INGREDIENTS

200 grams pineapple, cut into 1½-inch cubes

2 medium green capsicums, cut into 1½-inch pieces

2 medium onions, cut into 1½-inch pieces

2 medium tomatoes, seeded and cut into 1½-inch pieces

Salt to taste

2 teaspoons red chilli powder

1½ teaspoons powdered dried fenugreek leaves

2 teaspoons *garam masala* powder

1 teaspoon *chaat masala*

2 tablespoons vinegar

1 tablespoon oil

METHOD

- In a bowl, mix together the salt, chilli powder, powdered fenugreek leaves, *garam masala* powder, *chaat masala*, vinegar and oil.
- Add the pineapple and vegetables, and mix thoroughly. Set aside to marinate for one hour.
- Thread the pineapple, capsicum, onion and tomato one after the other onto toothpicks. Pour the remaining marinade on top.
- Heat a non-stick *tawa*; place the toothpicks on it and cook over medium heat, turning the toothpicks a few times so that the vegetables cook evenly on all sides. Cook till lightly-coloured.
- Serve hot with a salad and chutney.

Non-Stick Tawa

DHANIA PUDINA PARANTHA

INGREDIENTS

1/4 cup finely chopped fresh coriander

1/4 cup finely chopped fresh mint

2 cups wholewheat flour

Salt to taste

1/2 cup yogurt

2 teaspoons *chaat masala*

1/2 cup yogurt

METHOD

- Place the flour and salt in a bowl. Add the chopped coriander and mint, and knead into a soft dough with a little water. Cover and rest the dough for twenty to twenty-five minutes.
- Divide the dough into eight equal portions. Shape them into balls. Mix together the yogurt and *chaat masala*.
- Roll out each ball into a medium-sized *chapati*. Spread a tablespoon of the yogurt mixture over the *chapati*.
- Fold the *chapati* like a fan and roll the fan up to form a disc. Set aside for five minutes.
- Roll out each disc into a five to seven-inch round *parantha*.

- Cook on a hot non-stick *tawa* till both sides are lightly golden brown.
- Before serving, crush the *parantha* lightly between your palms to open out the layers.

Chef's Tip: If you are cooking *Dhania Pudina Parantha* in the *tandoor*, apply a little water on the side that will stick to the *tandoor* wall.

BABY BAJRA ROTI

INGREDIENTS

2 cups millet flour

Salt to taste

4 tablespoons white butter (optional)

METHOD

- Heat two or three cups of water in a pan till lukewarm.
- Combine one-fourth of the millet flour and salt to taste, and knead with lukewarm water to make a semi-hard dough. Roll into a ball.
- Wet your hands and pat the ball of dough into a *roti*.
- Heat a non-stick *tawa* on medium heat and place the *roti* on it.
- Cook on one side and flip it over. Cook till the *roti* puffs up.
- Remove from the heat and serve hot with butter. Repeat the process to make the rest of the *roti*.

SPICY RAJMA PARANTHA

INGREDIENTS

⅓ cup red kidney beans

1 cup wholewheat flour

2 tablespoons soya flour

1 teaspoon red chilli powder

3-4 green chillies, finely chopped

½ teaspoon dried pomegranate seeds, ground

8-10 mint leaves, finely chopped

2 tablespoons tomato purée

Salt to taste

2 teaspoons oil

METHOD

- Soak the kidney beans overnight, or for at least six hours. Pressure-cook in two cups of salted water till soft.
- Drain thoroughly, cool and mash well. Reserve the cooking liquid.
- Mix the flour, soya flour, mashed kidney beans, chilli powder, green chillies, ground pomegranate seeds, chopped mint, tomato purée and salt to taste.
- Add the reserved cooking liquid, if necessary, and knead into a soft pliable dough.

- Cover with a damp cloth and set aside for fifteen minutes.
- Divide into eight to ten equal portions and shape them into balls.
- Roll out each portion into five to six-inch rounds. Brush a little oil on a hot non-stick *tawa* and place a *parantha* on it.
- Cook on medium heat for half a minute on each side. Lower the heat and cook till both sides are slightly brown.
- Serve hot, with fresh yogurt.

VARQI PARANTHA

INGREDIENTS

4 cups refined flour

1 cup milk

$2\frac{1}{2}$ teaspoons sugar

Salt to taste

$\frac{3}{4}$ cup pure ghee+ for shallow-frying

METHOD

- Warm the milk slightly and dissolve the sugar in it.
- Sift the flour with the salt. Make a well in the centre of the flour; pour in the milk and about half a cup of water.
- Mix into the flour gradually and knead into a soft dough. Cover with a damp cloth and set aside for ten minutes.
- Melt the ghee and add two-third of it to the dough, incorporating it gradually; knead again. Cover the dough and set aside for ten minutes.
- Place the dough on a lightly-floured surface and flatten with a rolling pin into a rectangular shape.
- Apply one-fourth of the remaining ghee evenly over the rolled dough, dust with the flour, fold one end over two-third of

the rectangle, and then fold the other end over it to make three folds.

- Cover and refrigerate for ten minutes. Repeat this process thrice. Roll the dough into a one-eighth inch thick rectangle and cut out four-inch circles with a cutter.
- Make three crisscross evenly spaced incisions on the surface of each *parantha*. Place the *paranthe* on greaseproof paper and refrigerate until ready to cook.
- Heat a non-stick *tawa*; add the ghee and cook the *paranthe* over low heat until golden brown on both sides. Serve immediately.

Chef's Tip: The longer you refrigerate the dough, the flakier the *parantha*. However do not refrigerate the dough for more than eight hours.

SANJORI

INGREDIENTS

Pastry

1½ cups refined flour

A pinch of salt

3 tablespoons oil

Pure ghee, as required

Filling

1 cup fine semolina

2 teaspoons ghee

1½ cups sugar

¾ cup milk

½ teaspoon green cardamom powder

METHOD

- Mix together the flour and salt. Add the oil and sufficient water and knead into a soft dough.
- Keep it covered with a damp cloth for at least one to two hours.
- For the filling, heat the ghee in a non-stick *kadai* and lightly roast the semolina. Add the sugar and stir.
- Mix the milk with three-fourth cup of water and add to the semolina mixture.
- Cook, stirring continuously, till the moisture is absorbed and the mixture forms a soft ball.

- Take the *kadai* off the heat, add the cardamom powder and mix well.
- Set aside to cool and divide into medium lemon-sized balls. Divide the dough also into the same number of portions.
- Grease the palms of your hands, flatten one portion of dough, place a ball of the semolina mixture in the centre, and bring the edges of the dough together to enclose the filling.
- Flatten slightly, and roll out as thinly as possible, using some flour to dust the surface only if required.
- Heat a non-stick *tawa* and dry-roast the sanjori on medium heat, till little light brown spots appear on both sides.
- Serve hot with ghee.

INSTANT UTTAPPAM

INGREDIENTS

1 cup fine semolina

1 cup yogurt

Salt to taste

$^1/_4$ teaspoon soda bicarbonate

1 medium onion, chopped

1 medium green capsicum, seeded and chopped

Red chilli powder, to taste

Crushed roasted cumin seeds, to taste

METHOD

- Place the semolina in a bowl with yogurt and salt. Mix well and set aside for fifteen minutes. Add half a cup of water and soda bicarbonate, and mix again.
- Heat a non-stick *tawa* and pour a ladleful of batter in the centre. Do not spread the batter. Sprinkle the onion, capsicum, chilli powder and cumin seeds over the *uttappam* and allow to cook on moderate heat.
- When the underside has cooked, flip over and cook the other side till set. Serve hot.

TIL MOONGPHALI ALOO

INGREDIENTS

1 tablespoon sesame seeds

2 tablespoons peanuts, coarsely crushed

750 grams baby potatoes

Salt to taste

1½ tablespoons oil

1 teaspoon cumin seeds

4 green chillies, chopped

1 inch ginger, chopped

1 tablespoon garlic paste

1 teaspoon roasted cumin powder

1 teaspoon red chilli powder

1½ tablespoons grated fresh coconut

1 teaspoon *garam masala* powder

2 teaspoons lemon juice

2 tablespoons chopped fresh coriander

METHOD

- Parboil the unpeeled potatoes in salted water in a deep non-stick pan and set aside. Press them lightly.
- Heat the oil in a non-stick *kadai* on medium heat; add the cumin seeds, green chillies and ginger.

- When the seeds begin to change colour, add the garlic paste and sauté for two or three minutes.
- Add the potatoes and toss well. Add the sesame seeds, peanuts, roasted cumin powder, chilli powder, coconut and *garam masala* powder. Adjust the salt.
- Continue to cook for five minutes, tossing continuously. Stir in the lemon juice.
- Serve hot, garnished with the chopped coriander.

STIR-FRIED VEGETABLE WRAPS

INGREDIENTS

4 sheets of rice paper

1 teaspoon oil

2 spring onions, chopped

½ cup chopped water chestnuts

½ inch ginger, minced

2 tablespoons soy sauce

1 teaspoon red chilli sauce

1 tablespoon rice vinegar

½ cup bean sprouts

2 tablespoons plum sauce, for dipping

METHOD

- Soak the rice papers in water for one minute before using.
- Heat the oil in a non-stick wok or *kadai* and stir-fry the spring onions and water chestnuts for about two minutes on medium heat.
- Add the ginger, soy sauce, chilli sauce and rice vinegar.
- Stir-fry for another two minutes ensuring that the vegetables remain crunchy and are not overcooked.
- Add the bean sprouts and stir-fry for another minute.
- Divide this mixture into four portions and place a portion on each sheet of rice paper. Roll up tightly.
- Serve immediately, with plum sauce.

DHAABE KI SABZIYAN

INGREDIENTS

10-12 cauliflower florets

2 medium potatoes, boiled and cut into 1-inch cubes

½ cup shelled green peas

½ teaspoon turmeric powder

3 tablespoons oil

½ teaspoon cumin seeds

5-6 garlic cloves, grated

2 medium onions, grated

2 medium tomatoes, grated

1½ teaspoons grated ginger

2 teaspoons coriander powder

½ teaspoon roasted cumin powder

1½ teaspoon red chilli powder

2 tablespoons chopped fresh coriander

Salt to taste

1 teaspoon *garam masala* powder

Dal-fry

1 cup split pigeon peas

1 teaspoon butter

½ teaspoon cumin seeds

½ teaspoon red chilli powder

5-6 garlic cloves, grated

METHOD

- Boil the cauliflower in one cup of water with a quarter spoon of turmeric powder in a non-stick pan for two to three minutes. Drain and set aside.
- Boil the green peas in one cup of water in a non-stick pan. Drain and refresh in cold water. Drain and set aside.
- Heat two tablespoons of oil in a non-stick *kadai* and sauté the boiled cauliflower and the potato cubes till golden brown. Drain on absorbent paper and set aside.
- Add one tablespoon of oil to the same non-stick *kadai* and add the cumin seeds. When they change colour, add the garlic and sauté till reddish brown.
- Add the onions and continue to sauté till brown. Add the tomatoes, ginger, remaining turmeric powder, coriander powder, roasted cumin powder and chilli powder. Sauté till the oil rises to the surface. Remove from the heat and set aside.
- For the *dal*-fry, soak the split pigeon peas in two cups of water for half

an hour. Drain; boil with three cups of water till done.

- In another non-stick pan, heat the butter and add the cumin seeds, chilli powder, garlic and half the prepared gravy.
- Mix and add the boiled *dal* and salt to taste; bring to a boil. Simmer for two to three minutes.
- Add half the chopped coriander. Add the boiled peas, sautéed potatoes and cauliflower to the remaining gravy.
- Mix well and cook on low heat for two to three minutes. Add the remaining chopped coriander.
- Sprinkle the *garam masala* powder and serve.

PANEER KHURCHAN

INGREDIENTS

250 grams cottage cheese, cut into thick strips

1 tablespoon oil

1 teaspoon cumin seeds

2 teaspoons garlic paste

2 medium green capsicums, cut into thick strips

2 medium tomatoes, seeded and cut into thick strips

2 medium onions, cut into thick strips

3 tablespoons tomato purée

Salt to taste

1 teaspoon red chilli powder

1 teaspoon lemon juice

1 teaspoon dried fenugreek leaves, roasted and crushed

METHOD

- Heat the oil in a non-stick *kadai*; add the cumin seeds.
- When they begin to change colour, add the garlic paste, capsicums, tomatoes and onions, and sauté on medium heat for five or six minutes.
- Add the cottage cheese, tomato purée, salt and chilli powder.
- Sauté for a while till the cottage cheese begins to stick to the *kadai*.
- Scrape the cottage cheese off the bottom of the *kadai* and sauté for a while longer till the cottage cheese is dark brown and mashed.
- Stir in the lemon juice and dried fenugreek leaves.
- Serve immediately.

SUBZ LAJAWAB

INGREDIENTS

15-18 French beans, cut into ½-inch pieces

3 medium carrots, cut into ½-inch pieces

2 medium green capsicums, cut into ½-inch pieces

¼ medium cauliflower, separated into small florets

3 medium potatoes, boiled, and cut into ½-inch pieces

2 teaspoons oil

1 bay leaf

¾ cup boiled onion paste

2 green chillies, slit

2 teaspoons coriander powder

Salt to taste

2 teaspoons red chilli powder

3 tablespoons tomato purée

½ teaspoon green cardamom powder

METHOD

- Heat the oil in a non-stick *kadai* and add the bay leaf.
- When it begins to change colour, add the onion paste and sauté over low

heat till the oil separates. Do not brown the paste.

- Add the green chillies, coriander powder, salt and chilli powder, and sauté for two minutes.
- Add the tomato purée and cook for another three or four minutes. Add the French beans, carrots, capsicums, cauliflower and potatoes.
- Cover and cook over low heat for eight to ten minutes, till cooked.
- Stir in the cardamom powder and serve hot.

STIR-FRIED MEDLEY

INGREDIENTS

150 grams extra-firm bean curd, cut into ½-inch cubes

4-5 broccoli florets

1 tablespoon sliced celery

1 medium green capsicum, sliced

½ medium red capsicum, sliced

1 leek, sliced

3-4 fresh button mushrooms, sliced

2 garlic cloves

¼ inch ginger

¾ tablespoon oil

2 tablespoons roasted peanuts, crushed

1 tablespoon soy sauce

1 tablespoon tomato sauce

A dash of red chilli sauce

1½ teaspoons lemon juice

1½ teaspoons cornflour

½ cup fresh pineapple chunks

METHOD

- Pound the garlic and ginger to a paste. Heat the oil in a non-stick *kadai* and sauté the ginger-garlic paste and bean curd till lightly browned. Drain and set aside.

- To the same *kadai*, add the broccoli, celery, capsicums, leek, mushrooms and peanuts.
- Stir-fry till the vegetables are tender, but remain crisp.
- Mix together the soy sauce, tomato sauce, chilli sauce, lemon juice and cornflour. Add to the pan and cook, stirring continuously, till well mixed.
- Add the bean curd and pineapple, and mix gently. Serve hot with boiled rice.

NADIR YAKHNI

INGREDIENTS

500 grams lotus stems, cut into ¾-inch pieces

Salt to taste

2 tablespoons oil

2 medium onions, sliced

2 cups yogurt

1 tablespoon ghee

2 black cardamoms

4-6 cloves

2 inches cinnamon

1 teaspoon fennel powder

1 teaspoon dried ginger powder

4-6 green cardamoms

½ teaspoon caraway seeds

A big pinch of dried mint leaves, crushed

METHOD

- Bring four cups of water to a boil in a non-stick pan; add the lotus stems and salt, and cook till half done.
- Heat two tablespoons of oil in a non-stick *kadai* and sauté the onions on medium heat till brown.

- Cool and grind the onions, with a little water if necessary, to a smooth paste.
- Mix the yogurt with half a cup of water and strain through a piece of muslin.
- Cook the strained mixture on high heat, stirring continuously, till the mixture changes colour. Remove from the heat.
- Heat the ghee in a non-stick *kadai*; add the black cardamoms, cloves and cinnamon, and sauté till the spices sizzle.
- Mix the fennel powder and dried ginger powder in one cup of water. Add the browned onion paste and mix well.
- Add the mixture to the pan and stir. Add the cooked yogurt and lotus stems, and mix well.
- Add the salt and green cardamoms. Cook till the lotus stems are tender.
- Add the caraway seeds and dried mint. Stir and remove from the heat.
- Serve hot.

BURNT GINGER RICE

INGREDIENTS

4 inches ginger, thinly sliced

1 cup rice

2 tablespoons oil

1 small onion, finely chopped

1 tablespoon soy sauce

½ tablespoon tomato sauce

½ tablespoon red chilli paste

¼ teaspoon MSG (optional)

Salt to taste

2 tablespoons chopped fresh coriander

1 teaspoon vinegar

METHOD

- Soak the rice in four to five cups of water for one hour. Cook in four cups of boiling water until just cooked. Drain and cool.
- Heat the oil in a non-stick wok or *kadai*; add the ginger and stir-fry for two or three minutes, or till the ginger turns brown.
- Drain on absorbent paper. Reserve some ginger pieces for garnishing and finely chop the rest.
- Reheat the oil; add the chopped fried ginger and onion, and stir-fry for a few

seconds. Add the cooked rice, soy sauce, tomato sauce, red chilli paste, MSG and salt to taste.

- Cook over high heat for one minute, stirring and tossing continuously.
- Stir in the chopped coriander and vinegar, and serve hot, garnished with the reserved fried ginger slices.

HAKKA-STYLE RICE NOODLES

INGREDIENTS

150 grams rice noodles

Salt to taste

2 tablespoons oil

1 medium onion, sliced

1 small carrot, cut into thin strips

1 medium green capsicum, cut into thin strips

6-8 French beans, cut into thin strips

1/4 small cabbage, finely shredded

1 tablespoon light soy sauce

1/4 teaspoon MSG (optional)

1/4 teaspoon white pepper powder

1/2 cup bean sprouts

1 stalk spring onion greens, cut into fine long strips

METHOD

- Boil six cups of water in a deep non-stick pan. Add the salt and one tablespoon of oil.
- Add the noodles, take the pan off the heat, cover and leave to stand for three minutes.

- Drain the noodles, refresh in cold water and drain again. Spread on a large plate to cool.
- Heat the remaining oil in a non-stick wok; add the onion and stir-fry for two minutes.
- Add the carrot, green capsicum, French beans and cabbage, and stir-fry for two minutes, stirring and tossing continuously.
- Add the noodles, soy sauce, MSG, salt to taste and white pepper powder; cook on high heat for a couple of minutes, tossing continuously, until the noodles are heated through.
- Add the bean sprouts, mix well and serve hot, garnished with the spring onion greens.

QUICK STIR-FRIED NOODLES

INGREDIENTS

200 grams eggless noodles

Salt to taste

2 tablespoons oil

1 medium onion, sliced

1 medium carrot, cut into thin strips

¼ medium cabbage, shredded

1 medium green capsicum, cut into thin strips

2 stalks spring onion greens, sliced diagonally

1½ tablespoons light soy sauce

1 cup bean sprouts

1 teaspoon sesame oil

METHOD

- Boil the noodles in a deep non-stick pan in six to eight cups of salted water to which one tablespoon of oil has been added; cook till almost done.
- Drain, refresh in cold water and drain again. Spread on a large plate to cool. Heat the remaining oil in a non-stick wok or *kadai*, to smoking point.

- Add the onion and stir-fry for one minute. Add the carrot, cabbage and green capsicum, and stir-fry for two to three minutes.
- Add the noodles and salt; stir and toss for one more minute.
- Add the spring onion greens and soy sauce and toss again. Add the bean sprouts and toss well to mix.
- Transfer the noodles to a serving bowl, sprinkle the sesame oil over.
- Serve immediately.

ANNEXURE

- **CORIANDER AND MINT CHUTNEY**

  Grind together 1 cup fresh coriander, ½ cup fresh mint, 2-3 green chillies, black salt to taste, ¼ teaspoon sugar and 1 tablespoon lemon juice to a smooth paste using a little water if required

- **TAMARIND PULP**

  Soak 75 grams tamarind in 100 ml warm water for 10-15 minutes. Grind to a smooth paste and strain to remove any fibres. Store in an airtight container in the refrigerator.

- **VEGETABLE STOCK**

  Peel, wash and chop 1 onion, ½ medium carrot, 2-3 inch celery stalk and 2-3 garlic cloves. Place in a pan with 1 bay leaf, 5-6 peppercorns, 2-3 cloves and 5 cups of water and bring to a boil. Lower heat and simmer for 15 minutes and strain. Cool and store in a refrigerator till further use.

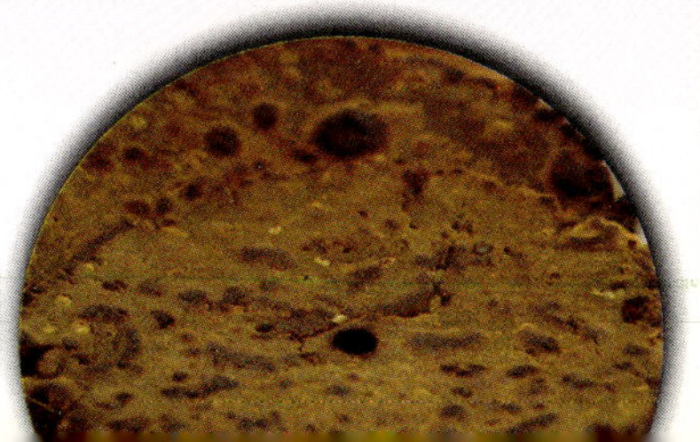

GLOSSARY

ENGLISH	HINDI
Basil leaves	Tulsi ke patte
Black Bengal gram	Kale chane
Caraway seeds	Shahi jeera
Cardamoms, green	Elaichi
Cinnamon	Dalchini
Cottage cheese	Paneer
Dried fenugreek leaves	Kasoori methi
Dried ginger powder	Saunth
Fennel seeds	Saunf
Gram, Bengal split	Chana dal
Gram, black skinless split	Dhuli urad dal
Gram, black split	Chilkewali urad dal
Lotus roots	Kamal kakdi/bhen
Millet	Bajra
Mushrooms	Khumb
Olive	Jaitun
Pine nuts	Chilgoza
Pomegranate seeds, dried	Anardana
Red kidney beans	Rajma
Vinegar	Sirka
Water chestnut	Singhara